LILLENAS®
DRAMA

Take 5

Comic Scripts in 5 Minutes or Less

By TORRY MARTIN

Lillenas® PUBLISHING COMPANY

KANSAS CITY, MO 64141

    Lillenas Publishing Company
    Drama Resources
    P.O. Box 419527
    Kansas City, MO 64141
    Phone: 816-931-1900 * Fax: 816-412-8390
    E-mail: drama@lillenas.com
    Web site: www.lillenasdrama.com

Cover art byPaul Franitza

Dedication

To my beloved spiritual parents and mentors,
Pastor Jack and Ann Aiken.
Thank you for equipping me and sending me out on this incredible journey.
P.S. Next time give me a map.

Contents

Acknowledgments 7

Preface 9

The Impertinence of Being Ernestine (Loving your neighbor, prayer) ...11

Precious Moments (Accepting responsibility, passing judgment)...........16

Take Five (Prayer, dealing with stress) 20

A Dramatic Dilemma (Being prepared) 24

Getting It Together (Evangelism, reaching out to others) 26

Rain Men (False boasting)..31

The Weekend of Our Discontent (Importance of reading
   the Bible, encouraging each other)..35

Addicted, to You (Judging others)...41

Knowing You (God knows us) 45

Acknowledgments

I wish to thank . . .

Robert Austin Browning, for being a role model to me and for being the best friend I could ever ask for. Thanks for making the good times great and the bad times better. (Even though you were largely responsible for both. Ha!)

My terrific parents, William and Verna Martin, who believed in me and encouraged me to march to my own drumbeat, even though they are both fully aware that I have no rhythm and am completely tone deaf which makes following a drumbeat impossible.

My trusted friends, Martha Bolton, Gail Rizzo, Russell Grove, Loren Kelly, Elizabeth Gibson, Lauren Yarger, Thomas Leo, and Jennifer Leo. Your combined insights and ideas have been most helpful in the writing of these sketches. I appreciate all of you more than words can say and I'm so thankful you are all in my life. Now you each owe me dinner, but no fast food.

Chris Rosetti and Juanita Aranda at WYSIWYG Filmworks for making the sketch *Take Five* read accurately and make sense.

The entire staff at Adventures in Odyssey, particularly Chris McDonald, Nathan Hoobler, John Fornof, Marshal Younger, Bob Hoose, Kathy Wierenga, Paul McCusker, Chuck Bolte, and Jonathan Crowe. You are all my second family and I am honored to be among you. I'm just crazy about you guys and appreciate all that you do for me.

Kim Messer, for being a wonderful editor and a terrific friend. I say those things freely by the way with no gun to my head—because we don't like guns, do we? Heh-heh. (The only thing more fun than teasing a friend is needling an editor!)

The Lillenas Dramatic Company—Chris Todd, Heather Tinker, Chad and Stacey Schnarr. You guys are the most talented actors I know and you all have been a wonderful source of encouragement and inspiration. It's an honor to have you perform my sketches. You make them soooo much better!

The many people who attend the Lillenas Drama Conference and have become my friends over the years. You are some of the most amazing people I've ever met. Thank you for being so bold in your proclamation of the Gospel and for doing it with such joy and conviction.

Preface

You might have noticed that this book is dedicated to my Pastor, Jack Aiken and his wonderful wife, Ann. Some of the sketches in the book you are holding can be directly traced back to a class I took under Ann's teaching, so I thought it might be interesting for the reader to learn how those sketches came to be. In particular, I am referring to the "It Just Makes Sense" sketches which are dramatic illustrations of scriptures.

The class in Alaska that Ann was teaching was one of Kay Arthur's Precept Bible Ministry studies for the book of 2 Peter. I was amazed at some of the things I was learning, and I loved doing the word studies. We would do an in-depth look at the original Greek and Hebrew texts of the Bible, and some of the things I was learning would just blow my mind. Apparently, however, it's pretty easy for others to recognize when a Bible truth is being revealed to me because my face readily registers excitement and awe. (I have always been told that I wear my heart on my sleeve, so it's well known that I'm not very good at covering my emotions.)

Anyway, whenever Ann would notice a scriptural truth sinking into my mind and heart she would look at me and smile while saying; "It just makes sense now, doesn't it, Torry? The Bible . . . it just makes sense." And you know what? It does! The Bible makes complete sense, and I honestly don't see how people can claim that it's confusing. Being aware of that "the Bible is difficult" excuse however, I set out to create a series of sketches that would illustrate how easy the Bible is to understand and how it makes perfect sense to live by the principals God has presented us with. My goal was to hopefully encourage people to start reading their own Bibles more and to realize that it's not a difficult thing to grasp. And that, dear reader, is how the "It Just Makes Sense" sketches were born. I encourage all of you to read your Bibles, by the way, and also, if you ever have the opportunity to take a Precept Ministry class, jump on it! The Bible will come alive to you and change your life. In fact, I'm hoping one day to meet Kay Arthur personally so I can explain to her the profound impact her studies have made on me and how they have shaped my life and career. If any of you know her, however, please feel free to tell her that for me and mention also that she owes me a lunch for the free publicity. Anything fried will be fine.

By the way, on the topic of sketch origination, two of the most frequently asked questions I receive as a Christian comedian and author are, "Where do you get your comedy material from?" and "Where do you come up with the ideas for your comedy sketches?" To conclude my preface, I will now attempt to give a written answer for both.

The truth is that the very best material for humor and sketch ideas comes from making real life observations. Because people say and do the most unintentionally ridiculous things, I've learned to carry a pocket tape recorder with me everywhere. (I also have chronic A.D.D. and a VERY short attention span. Therefore, the miniature tape recorder helps me to record my thoughts before I lose them.) I never know when I'll stumble across a comedic gem or a sketch idea so I have to take precautions to preserve them when I do. (NOTE: Show me a gifted slice-of-life comedian and what I'll show you is a very successful eavesdropper.)

The following story serves to better illustrate my point:

I was once in an airport gift shop in Anchorage, Alaska when I witnessed an interesting exchange between a couple who were obviously on their honeymoon. They were disagreeing in the most polite way possible about what souvenirs to get both of their mothers. Apparently the young woman had picked up a lovely trinket for her own mother a few days earlier on their vacation. But being a typical male, the young man had neglected to do any of his own souvenir gift shopping until the very last minute, therefore limiting himself to whatever was available in the airport gift shop. I was doing some shopping of my own in the store when I "accidentally" overheard a part of their conversation. Since I am always looking for new sketch material, I became intrigued by their discussion and decided to follow them around the store while I continued to listen, being careful not to draw any attention to myself.

I witnessed the groom picking up an object to purchase but his new wife questioned the financial fairness of it. "That costs more than what we got my mom," she said. "Yes, but my mom is nicer," he replied. She stared at him for a moment before saying, "Good. Then your mom can pay for your separate flight home." The conversation continued as I followed them unobtrusively while making mental notes.

When I felt I had gotten some pretty good lines for a future sketch, I headed straight to the bathroom and went in to a stall where I could tape record in private what I had observed. I was halfway through recording my version of their conversation when suddenly there was a loud "thump-thump-thump"—knocking sound against the divider from the stall wall next to me.

I was immediately startled and stopped talking into my tape recorder for a moment. The knocking had immediately ceased and I then heard a voice stating, "My name is Marcus and her name is April if it helps you in your story any." It was the newly wedded husband. I was completely embarrassed to be caught in such a compromising position, but meekly recorded the additional information onto my cassette recorder followed by a quickly stated thanks to the man on the other side. I then made a rather hasty exit from the porcelain chamber.

My purpose in sharing this story is to hopefully educate any would-be comedians or comedy sketch writers who may be among my readers.

Comedy Lesson Number One: Listen, observe, and record, but don't get caught with your pants down.

It just makes sense.

The Impertinence of Being Ernestine

Running Time: 5 minutes

Theme: Loving your neighbor, prayer, living at peace

Scripture References: "For the whole law is fulfilled in one word, in the statement, 'You shall love your neighbor as yourself.'" Galatians 5:14
"Do not devise harm against your neighbor, while he lives securely beside you." Proverbs 3:29

Cast:
> ERNESTINE O'RILEY—An elderly Christian lady with a short temper and no patience
> LIONEL FRANKLIN—Young Christian man who is generally likable and tries hard to get along with others, patient to a point

Setting: Living room setting for Ernestine. Office setting for Lionel.

Props:
> 2 telephones
> Lounge chair
> End table
> Desk with pencil and note pad for doodling
> Desk chair
> Coat rack

Costumes: Ernestine wears a loud flowered muumuu with a matching turban. Lionel is wearing a striped shirt with plaid pants and a Betty Boop tie and a coat.

(Both actors stay completely on opposite sides of the stage. They are in two different settings so they should never look at each other onstage. ERNESTINE enters SR and holds her wireless phone to her ear with one hand while carrying a glass of water with the other. She has been put on hold and is losing patience. She gets seated on her cushioned chair and sets her glass of water down on the end table next to it.)

ERNESTINE: Come on, someone, and answer the phone! I've been on hold for five minutes and I'm not getting any younger!

LIONEL *(runs on SL and tries to hang up his coat but it falls off the coat rack twice. He finally decides to drape the entire coat rack with his coat using his jacket as a covering)*: Oh great, I can already tell that it's going to be one of those days. *(Hurriedly sits at desk, picking up phone receiver and pressing button to take waiting call; a little out of breath)* City Hall. Lionel Franklin speaking.

11

ERNESTINE: It's about time someone answered! I've been waiting so long I almost died of thirst! Had to go get me some water!

LIONEL: I'm sorry about that, ma'am, but I'm here now. What can I do for you?

ERNESTINE: I don't know. Probably nothing, but we're gonna find out. My name is Ernestine Scott and I'd like to speak with someone about exchanging my neighbor.

LIONEL: I beg your pardon?

ERNESTINE: My neighbor. I'd like to exchange him for one that I like.

LIONEL: I'm sorry, but I don't think I can help you with that.

ERNESTINE: Why not? This is City Hall isn't it? I pay my taxes!

LIONEL: Ma'am, I'd love to be of service, but we don't have an exchanging neighbor's department.

ERNESTINE: Oh. What about having him evicted instead?

LIONEL: Are you the person's landlord?

ERNESTINE: No.

LIONEL: Then I'm afraid that I can't help you with an eviction process either.

ERNESTINE: OK then, how much trouble could I get in if I just moved him myself?

LIONEL: What?

ERNESTINE: You heard me! If I waited until he went to work and then I moved him out while he was gone. How much trouble?

LIONEL: I'd say quite a bit. You'd probably be charged with trespassing, then you'd be charged with burglary, and vandalism, along with a possible charge for destruction of personal property if anything was damaged.

ERNESTINE: Uh-huh, and how much would that cost?

LIONEL: I beg your pardon?

ERNESTINE: If I was charged with all of it. I have a $1,500.00 limit on my credit card and I get a service fee if I go over. So how much?

LIONEL: Ma'am, I'm not talking about credit card charges, I'm talking about legal charges that could send you to prison.

ERNESTINE: Prison? Well at least there I'd have new neighbors.

LIONEL: Yes, but I've got a feeling you wouldn't like them either.

ERNESTINE: Probably not.

LIONEL: Ma'am, just out of curiosity, have you ever tried talking to your neighbor about whatever he's doing that bothers you?

ERNESTINE: That's exactly the problem. He won't talk to me! He's lived there for over a month now and he won't even say hi.

LIONEL: He certainly doesn't sound very friendly.

ERNESTINE: Not at all, and I've been trying to be a good Christian about the whole thing, but my neighbor's making me so mad that I can't.

LIONEL: You can't be a good Christian?

ERNESTINE: It's not my fault! It's the neighbors!

LIONEL (*slightly confused*): I'm not sure I'm following.

ERNESTINE: Oh brother. Look, the Bible says to love my neighbor as myself, right?

LIONEL: Right.

ERNESTINE: Well, I love myself just fine. That's not a problem. But how can I be expected to love a neighbor who every morning when I get my newspaper off the porch won't even say hi to me?

LIONEL (*trying to be nice*): I understand that's . . . difficult.

ERNESTINE: Difficult? It makes me so boiling mad I actually start wishing harmful things on my neighbor!

LIONEL: Oh.

ERNESTINE: And brother, that's not being a good Christian. So in order for me to stay right with the Lord, that neighbor has got to go!

LIONEL: I see. Well, ma'am, I'm a Christian too so believe me, I know all about how hard it is to love your neighbor but . . .

ERNESTINE: But what?

LIONEL: But . . . if you don't mind my saying, there are a lot worse things a neighbor could do than simply not to say hi.

ERNESTINE: Oh yeah? Like what?

LIONEL: Well, I don't know. (*Beat*) Like staring for starters.

ERNESTINE: Staring?

LIONEL: Yeah. See, I just moved into a new neighborhood myself and I've got a neighbor who doesn't do anything but stare at me every morning. It sort of creeps me out.

ERNESTINE: Does it make you feel like a bad Christian too?

LIONEL: It did until I decided to stop being mad at my neighbor and start praying for her instead.

ERNESTINE: You pray for your neighbor?

LIONEL: Yep, and believe it or not, it makes me feel better about both of us.

ERNESTINE: So it's working then, is it?

LIONEL: I think so and who knows, one day my neighbor and I might even become friends. You might want to give it a try yourself.

ERNESTINE: Praying, huh? I probably should have thought of that. I suppose it couldn't hurt anything.

LIONEL: And not hurting anything is important. You seem like a nice lady so I'd hate for you to do something drastic about your neighbor and then get into trouble or end up in jail.

ERNESTINE: Trust me, I'd hate to end up in jail too. Orange jumpsuits are so unflattering.

LIONEL: True, *(laughs)* but even that would be an improvement over the outfits my bad neighbor usually wears.

ERNESTINE: What do you mean?

LIONEL: Oh, her entire wardrobe consists of nothing but flower-covered muumuus and matching turbans. *(Laughs)*

ERNESTINE *(looks at her own outfit, adjusts her turban, and clears throat)*: What's wrong with that? Sounds fashionable to me.

LIONEL: It probably was . . . in the 60s. *(Laughs)*

ERNESTINE: Well, at least your bad neighbor doesn't wear plaids with stripes like mine.

LIONEL: Pardon?

ERNESTINE: He wears plaid with stripes! *(Laughs)* Then he tops it off with some hideously ugly Betty Boop tie. *(Laughs)* Must have an entire collection of those things.

LIONEL *(looks at his own outfit, touches his tie, and clears throat)*: Actually, I've heard that Betty Boop ties are quite popular.

ERNESTINE: They probably were . . . in the 40s. *(Laughs)*

LIONEL: Ma'am. I know this is going to sound odd, but exactly where do you live?

ERNESTINE: 222 Love Road. Why?

LIONEL: Because I live at 224 Love Road.

ERNESTINE: Oh, my word.

LIONEL: We're neighbors.

ERNESTINE: You're the Betty Boop Boy?

LIONEL: And you're the Muumuu Turban Lady.

ERNESTINE *(yells angrily)*: Why on earth don't you ever say hi?

LIONEL *(defensive)*: Because you're always staring at me!

ERNESTINE *(yelling)*: I'm staring cause I'm waiting for you to say hi!

LIONEL *(quietly)*: Oh. *(Pauses in shock and says while being flustered)* Hi.

ERNESTINE: Well, hello there! *(Beat)* See, now wasn't that easy?

LIONEL: Yes. Yes it was. *(Laughs nervously, tries to be confidently friendly)* Care to take it to the next level?

ERNESTINE: What do you mean?

LIONEL *(clears throat and says cheerfully)*: And how are you today, neighbor?

ERNESTINE *(instantly angry)*: How I am is none of your concern you little weasel!

LIONEL *(shocked)*: I beg your pardon?

ERNESTINE: I don't want a neighbor who goes poking around in all my business. I just want one that says hi. *(Slams phone down)* Nosey neighbor! *(Exits, stomping off angrily)*

LIONEL *(stunned, hangs up slowly)*: I think loving my neighbor is going to take a little more prayer.

(Exits)

Precious Moments

An "It Just Makes Sense" Sketch

Running Time: 5 minutes

Theme: Accepting responsibility, meddling with others, passing judgment

Scripture Reference: "Like one who takes a dog by the ears is he who passes by and meddles with strife not belonging to him." Proverbs 26:17

Cast:

CONSTANCE—Emotional mother who lashes out in desperate moments
VINCENT—Father who tries to keep it together, fed up accepting blame
MIKE—Man in the park, trying to mind his own business but failing
NARRATOR

Setting: A park

Props:

2 park benches
Crutches

Costumes: Contemporary clothing

(CONSTANCE *runs on from SL crying. She sits on the bench and sobs quietly.* MIKE *hobbles out on crutches from SR and sits on bench the opposite side of stage from her. He isn't too aware of her at first. Throughout this whole scene we should see* MIKE *being uncomfortable and trying not to pay attention. Eventually he becomes wrapped up in the story, however, as if he is watching a soap opera. He tries not to get caught eavesdropping.* VINCENT *enters and sits next to* CONSTANCE *while she cries.*)

VINCENT: Constance? (*She ignores him, turning away*) Constance, are you going to talk to me? (*Pause, sighing*) I don't see why you keep blaming me for this.

CONSTANCE: Because it's your fault. That's why.

VINCENT (*defensive*): My fault? How is it my fault?

CONSTANCE: You're the one who raised her.

VINCENT: Not by myself, I didn't. Why is it that every time she's good, she's yours, and when she's bad, she's mine?

CONSTANCE: Fine. We both raised her but you are the one who spoiled her.

VINCENT (*sitting down*): I'm her dad. I'm supposed to spoil her.

CONSTANCE: Not like that! Not the way you do! The last time she ran away she was gone for a week, and when she finally comes home what do you do instead of disciplining her? You reward her!

VINCENT: I know. I'm sorry. I just wanted her to appreciate how good she has it at home so she wouldn't leave again.

CONSTANCE: Well, it doesn't seem to have worked, does it? She's gone. She's gone and we don't know if she's ever coming back.

VINCENT *(sighs)*: She'll be back. *(Beat)* You spoiled her too, you know.

CONSTANCE: No, I didn't.

VINCENT: Who buys her those outfits? I sure don't. In fact, if it were up to me, I wouldn't even let her go outside the way she dresses. All those miniskirts, midriffs, and leopard skin coats. It's just looking for trouble.

CONSTANCE: I'll have you know that she picks those outfits out herself. She picks them out and then throws a fit in the middle of the store if I don't buy them! There's nothing I can do about it.

VINCENT: How about telling her no, huh? How about that?

CONSTANCE: I do tell her no but she doesn't listen to me! You're the only one she listens to. You're the only one she obeys. I'm just the mother she takes for granted.

VINCENT: And I suppose that's my fault too?

CONSTANCE: Well, maybe if you disciplined her every once in a while she would listen to me. You're the man of the house. You're the one who should set her boundaries.

VINCENT: What am I supposed to do? Chain her to her bed? Lock her in her room? Build a high security fence around the house so she never leaves the yard? Huh? Are those the kind of boundaries you want?

CONSTANCE: Maybe so! At least then we'd know she was safe. *(Wipes nose)* I can't believe you thought coming to the park would be a good idea.

VINCENT: It's the only place we haven't looked and she loves it here. I was hoping we might find her or run into someone who knows her and can tell us where she is.

CONSTANCE *(pauses, looking around)*: We used to come here all the time as a family.

VINCENT: I know. *(Beat)* Remember how she loved going down that slide when she was little? She couldn't get enough. You used to hold her on your lap on the swings over there.

CONSTANCE: I miss those days. All they are now is precious memories. *(Sniffles and breaks down again)* Oh, Vincent, what if she never comes back?

VINCENT: She'll come back, honey. Trust me, it's not going to take long for her to realize that she can't make it by herself. We need to deal with this together, though, and stop blaming each other.

CONSTANCE (*sniffling*): I suppose you're right.

VINCENT: I know I am. It's the only way we're going to get through it. It's not either of our faults that she ran away.

MIKE: Actually, I think it is.

VINCENT: What?

MIKE (VINCENT *and* CONSTANCE *look at each other finding it hard to believe a stranger would be interfering in such a private matter*): Sorry, I couldn't help listening, but you weren't exactly being quiet. Anyway, from what I've seen of your situation so far, I think you're both to blame. You both spoiled her and neither of you set up boundaries or made sure she was disciplined. So like I said, it's both your faults.

VINCENT: You know, buddy, maybe it'd be better if you minded your own business.

CONSTANCE: I agree. This is a private matter and it doesn't involve strangers. And by the way, not everything that ever happens is always the parents' fault.

VINCENT: That's right. We're not the ones who taught her to tear up furniture or to chase cars and jump fences.

CONSTANCE: We didn't teach her to run away or bark at mailmen either. She does all those things herself.

MIKE: Wait a minute? Are you talking about a dog?

CONSTANCE: Of course we are!

VINCENT: What else would we be talking about?

MIKE: Good grief. I thought all the drama was about something that really mattered, not a dog. I hate dogs!

(CONSTANCE *gasps.*)

VINCENT: How could anyone hate dogs?

MIKE: They're flea-ridden, fur-shedding, tick-covered messes that will turn on you in a moment, that's how! In fact, just yesterday I tried breaking up two stray dogs that were fighting right here in the park and when I grabbed them by their ears to separate them, they turned on me and both bit me right here on the leg. Now I'm nothing but stitches and crutches and it's those two lousy dogs' fault.

CONSTANCE: Actually, if you don't mind me saying, it's your own fault that you got bit. You should never grab a dog by the ears. A dog's ears are very sensitive, you know.

MIKE: Sensitive, huh? Well, it's too bad you aren't. Good grief. Caring more about a dog than an injured human being. Makes me glad I had those mutts sent to the pound.

CONSTANCE: You sent them to the dog pound?

MIKE: Yup, it was a matter of public safety so I made the call myself. I should have known the one dog was mentally unstable just by the way it was dressed up in that miniskirt and a leopard fur coat.

CONSTANCE: Leopard fur?

VINCENT: Miniskirt?

MIKE: Pathetic beast was probably as deranged as its owner.

CONSTANCE *(jumping up)*: Precious! That was our poodle, Precious!

VINCENT: Our Precious is at the pound?

CONSTANCE *(to* MIKE*)*: And you grabbed her ear? How'd you like it if I grabbed your ear? *(Grabs* MIKE*'s ear)* Huh? Do you like that? How's that feel? You beast!

VINCENT: Constance, no!

MIKE *(yelling)*: Ow! Let go! Let go!

*(*VINCENT *pulls* CONSTANCE *off* MIKE, *but she continues yelling at him.)*

CONSTANCE: I have half a mind to beat you with your own crutches!

VINCENT: Constance, stop it. We don't have time for this. We've got to get to the dog pound to save Precious!

CONSTANCE *(breathing heavy to* VINCENT*)*: You're right. Our baby needs us. *(To* MIKE.*)* But I'll be back if you even bruised one of her ears when you grabbed her.

MIKE *(holding hands over his ears in pain)*: Her ears? What about my ears!

CONSTANCE: I hope they ring for a week! It'll teach you to mind your own business. Dog hater!

VINCENT: Ear puller!

CONSTANCE: Canine fashion critic!

*(*VINCENT *and* CONSTANCE *exit while* MIKE *freezes on seat.* NARRATOR *quickly enters, stopping in front of* MIKE *and facing audience. He has his Bible open.)*

NARRATOR: Proverbs 26:17 says; "Like one who takes a dog by the ears is he who passes by and meddles with strife not belonging to him." *(Slams Bible shut)*

MIKE: The Bible . . . *(Grabs crutches)* it just makes sense.

(Beat, NARRATOR *helps* MIKE *to exit quickly.)*

Take Five

Running Time: 5 minutes

Theme: Importance of prayer, dealing with stress

Scripture References: "Devote yourselves to prayer, keeping alert in it with an attitude of thanksgiving." Colossians 4:2
". . . Casting all your anxiety upon him, because he cares for you." 1 Peter 5:7

Cast:
LAURA—Actress for the commercial shoot, very sweet but a little stressed
DIRECTOR—Amiable and professional
CAMERAMAN—Man of few words but nice
MAKEUP GIRL—Helpful and kind
CLAPPER—Professional and friendly

Setting: The Kingdom Network TV soundstage

Props:
Video camera
Light meter
Director's chair
Director's megaphone
Makeup kit with hairbrush
Handheld mirror
Clapboard
Small package of tissues for Makeup Girl

Costumes: Contemporary clothing

(Everyone but LAURA *enters at the same time. A* CAMERAMAN *sets up a tripod then takes out a light meter he holds upwards as if checking the light readings. The* MAKEUP GIRL *gets her stuff ready while the* CLAPPER *writes out the information about the shoot on his clapboard with chalk.* DIRECTOR *observes everything and briefly checks on the others' activities.)*

DIRECTOR: Has anyone seen Laura?

CLAPPER: I haven't.

CAMERAMAN: Nope

MAKEUP GIRL: I thought she was here already.

CLAPPER: Me too.

DIRECTOR: We can't very well shoot a public service announcement if we don't have our actress. Can someone call her at home?

MAKEUP GIRL: I'll do it. (*Starts to exit but is stopped by* LAURA.)

LAURA (*running onstage through audience*): I'm here! I'm here! I am so, so sorry that I'm late. Either my alarm clock didn't ring or my cat shut it off.

(MAKEUP GIRL *starts fixing* LAURA'*s hair and makeup. She gives* LAURA *a handheld mirror to check herself while she works on her.*)

DIRECTOR: Your cat knows how to shut off an alarm clock?

LAURA: No, but he likes to lie on it and sometimes he shuts it off by accident. I really am sorry.

DIRECTOR: No harm done. How are you feeling about the sides I sent you home with?

LAURA (*pointing to her head with confidence*): It's all up here. I stayed up late to study them so I've got the sides memorized.

DIRECTOR: Whew. That's a relief. I was afraid you were going to tell me that your dog ate your homework.

LAURA: Pardon?

DIRECTOR (*laughs*): It was a joke. Cat shut off alarm. Dog ate homework. (*No one is laughing but he shrugs it off.*) Aw, never mind. I'm just glad you're here. Are you ready to film this thing?

LAURA: Yep, I'm ready when you are. Let's do it!

DIRECTOR: OK everyone. Places!

LAURA (*to* MAKEUP GIRL *as she takes the mirror from* LAURA *and leaves*): Thanks.

DIRECTOR: Quiet on the set. Roll camera.

CAMERAMAN: Speed.

CLAPPER: Take Five to Pray. Roll 1, Scene 1, Take 1. Mark! (*Slaps clapboard slate*)

DIRECTOR: And action!

LAURA: Hi, I'm Laura Newberry and I'm glad you're watching the Kingdom Network. You know we all get flustrated and frustered in our lives. Oops!

DIRECTOR: Cut. (*Laughs*) Laura, it's frustrated and flustered.

LAURA (*laughs*): I know! Sorry about that. Got a little tongue-tied.

DIRECTOR: That's OK, let's try it again. Places! Quiet on the set. Roll camera.

CAMERAMAN: Speed.

CLAPPER: Take Five to Pray. Roll 1, Scene 1, Take 2. Mark! (*Slaps clapboard slate*)

LAURA: Hi. I'm Naura Lewberry . . . I mean Laura Newberry.

DIRECTOR: Cut!

LAURA: Good grief. I forgot my own name!

DIRECTOR: That's OK. It happens to the best of us, right, Richard?

CAMERAMAN: I'm Chris.

DIRECTOR: Exactly.

LAURA: Anyway, I'm sorry about that.

DIRECTOR: No worries. Is everything OK?

LAURA: Yes, it's just that I was running so late this morning I didn't have time to pray.

DIRECTOR: Kind of funny that that's what the commercial is about, isn't it?

LAURA: Ironic, actually.

DIRECTOR: Ready to try again?

LAURA: I think so.

DIRECTOR: Places! Quiet please. Roll camera.

CAMERAMAN: Speed.

CLAPPER: Take Five to Pray. Roll 1, Scene 1, Take 3. Mark! *(Slaps clapboard slate)*

DIRECTOR: And action!

LAURA: Hi, I'm Laura Newberry and I'm glad you're watching The Kingdom Network. You know we all get frustrated and flustered in our lives and sometimes it seems like there's no escape from the outside pressures this world brings. Well, whenever I feel overcome with worry or overstressed with responsibilities, I've learned to take five minutes and pray. You should try it yourself the next time you need to escape and recharge. Take five and pray. It'll make the difference in your day. *(Pauses then excitedly says)* Yay! I did it! *(Proud)* How was that?

DIRECTOR: It was fine, Laura, except your forehead looks a little sweaty.

LAURA: What?

DIRECTOR: I mean "shiny." Makeup! (MAKEUP GIRL *fixes* LAURA's *sweaty forehead.)* Sorry about that Laura.

LAURA *(laughs)*: That's OK. It's not your fault I'm sweating, I mean "shining." *(Laughs)* I was the one who woke up late and had to sprint to get here.

MAKEUP GIRL *(to* DIRECTOR *about* LAURA's *appearance)*: How's that?

DIRECTOR: She looks great. OK, I think everyone's ready this time. Let's try it again. Places! Quiet everybody. Roll camera.

CAMERAMAN: Speed.

CLAPPER: Take Five to Pray. Roll 1, Scene 1, Take 4. Mark! *(Slaps clapboard)*

DIRECTOR: And action!

LAURA: Hi, I'm Laura Newberry and I'm glad you're watching The Klingon Network. Oh!

(Everyone laughs.)

DIRECTOR: Cut!

LAURA: The Klingon Network? What am I saying! I don't even like *Star Trek.*

CAMERAMAN *(laughs)*: Hey, Laura. *(Makes a Vulcan salute/greeting signal with his hand)* Live long and prosper!

LAURA: It's more like die young and perspire. I'm sweating again.

(MAKEUP GIRL wipes LAURA's forehead.)

MAKEUP GIRL: You're doing great, Laura.

LAURA: You're being kind, thanks. I really do wish I had taken the time to pray this morning though.

DIRECTOR: OK, Laura, one more time. We'll get this public service announcement done early so you can go home. Places and quiet everyone. Roll camera, please.

CAMERAMAN: Speed.

CLAPPER: Take Five to Pray. Roll 1, Scene 1, Take 5.

(Before the CAMERAMAN can say "Mark," LAURA interrupts him.)

LAURA: Wait! *(To DIRECTOR.)* Can we really do that?

DIRECTOR: Do what?

LAURA: Take five to pray before we film this?

DIRECTOR: I don't see why not.

LAURA: I could really use it.

MAKEUP GIRL: Me too.

CLAPPER: Count me in.

CAMERAMAN: Ditto.

DIRECTOR: Then it's agreed. *(Beat)* OK, take five and pray people. Take five and pray!

(All exit.)

A Dramatic Dilemma

An "It Just Makes Sense" Sketch

Running Time: 1 minute

Theme: Being prepared

Scripture Reference: "Preach the Word; be prepared in season and out of season." 2 Timothy 4:2

Cast:
> BARB—A member of the drama team who is more in charge
> CATHY—Another member of the drama team; shy and feeling awkward
> NARRATOR

Setting: Church sanctuary

Costume: Contemporary church garb

Note: Change the names of the characters and use your actors' real names instead. It's funnier to your own congregation that way.

(BARB *enters stage nervously, looking around. She awkwardly arrives CS and speaks in a stage whisper to* CATHY, *seated in the front row, unaware that she was supposed to be in a sketch today.*)

BARB (*stage whisper*): Cathy! (CATHY *is actually looking at her church program and unaware that* BARB *is onstage.* BARB *still in stage whisper*) Cathy! (CATHY *is still unaware.* BARB *speaks her name very loudly now to catch* CATHY's *attention.*) CATHY! (CATHY *looks up and sees* BARB *gesturing wildly for her to come onstage, eagerly drawing her up there.* CATHY *comes up apprehensive and nervous about joining* BARB *onstage. They stand together looking at each other.* BARB *pauses while waiting for* CATHY *to say something.*) Well?

CATHY: Well, what?

BARB: Say your line.

CATHY: What line?

BARB: From the sketch.

CATHY: What sketch?

BARB: The sketch I gave you last week about being prepared to share the gospel!

CATHY: We're doing that today?

BARB: Yes!

CATHY (*turns to face audience*): Oops.

(*Both actors freeze onstage as* NARRATOR *quickly enters, stopping in front of them, facing audience. He has his Bible open.*)

NARRATOR: 2 Timothy 4:2 says; "Preach the Word; be prepared in season and out of season." (*Slams Bible shut*)

BARB (*loudly*): The Bible . . . (CATHY *is supposed to join her in saying the last line but she doesn't.* BARB *finishes the sentence while feeling awkward.*) it just makes . . . sense. (*Looks at* CATHY.) You were supposed to say that with me!

CATHY: I was?

BARB: In unison.

CATHY: Want to do it again?

BARB: No . . . let's just . . . you know . . . go.

CATHY: OK.

(NARRATOR *exits shaking his head disappointedly.* BARB *exits offstage and* CATHY *starts to follow her until she suddenly remembers that she was sitting in the audience. She turns around quickly to return back to her front row seat.*)

CATHY (*embarrassed and pointing to her seat in the front row*): I was sitting down here. (*Exits completely and takes her seat.*)

Getting It Together

Running Time: 5 minutes

Theme: Evangelism, reaching out to others

Scripture References: And He said to them, "Go into all the world and preach the gospel to all creation." Mark 16:15
Additional Scriptures: Matthew 10:27; Luke 24:47; 2 Timothy 4:2

Cast:
BILLY BOB—A country boy, more of a leader type
BOBBY RAY—Sincere but not as smart, a follower

Setting: Church stage

Props:
Bottle of Excedrin

Costumes: Modern wear

(Opens with BILLY BOB *and* BOBBY RAY *both discouraged, bored, and staring into space while sitting on a church pew. Finally they both sigh in unison.)*

BILLY BOB: I don't get it.

BOBBY RAY: Yep.

BILLY BOB: Don't get it at all.

BOBBY RAY: Yep.

BILLY BOB *(pause)*: I mean, I really don't get it.

BOBBY RAY *(understanding that* BILLY BOB *doesn't "get it" and tired of hearing him say it)*: I get it!

BILLY BOB: Oh, you don't get it either.

BOBBY RAY: Yes, I do!

BILLY BOB: What do you get?

BOBBY RAY: The fact that you don't get it.

BILLY BOB: Yes, but what don't I get?

BOBBY RAY: I don't know. *(Looks around)* Maybe ya don't get it that no one's here.

BILLY BOB: Oh brother! I get that no one's here. I can look around and get that. That don't take no genius to get.

BOBBY RAY: See, I told ya I got it.

BILLY BOB: I'm talking about not getting the reason why no one's here.

BOBBY RAY: Oh! Why they ain't here. (Pause) Shoot, I don't get that either.

BILLY BOB: That's what I said.

BOBBY RAY: Right. (Beat) But no one else here gets it so at least we ain't alone.

BILLY BOB: But that's the point! We are alone! There ain't no one else here for getting anything.

BOBBY RAY: That don't make sense. If there ain't no one here, how do you know if they're forgetting anything?

BILLY BOB: I'm not talking about "forgetting"—one word, I'm talking about "for getting"—two words.

BOBBY RAY: Oh. (Beat) What two words did ya forget?

BILLY BOB: Forget it.

BOBBY RAY: Hey! Ya remembered!

BILLY BOB: Bobby Ray, you're giving me a headache.

BOBBY RAY: Sorry.

BILLY BOB: Imbecile.

BOBBY RAY: No. (Reaching in his pocket) But I got me some Excedrin.

BILLY BOB: Oh brother. (Standing up) I mean look at this place. We done built us a whole new church. Bought the piano, the stained glass windows, the choir robes, and a pretty little pulpit. We even specialty ordered the pews!

BOBBY RAY (pause): And the padding.

BILLY BOB: What?

BOBBY RAY: The padding for the pews. We got that too. (Pauses while BILLY BOB looks at him.) Well, when you was listing things you didn't mention it, is all.

BILLY BOB: I mentioned the pews.

BOBBY RAY: So?

BILLY BOB: So that included the padding.

BOBBY RAY: But we were charged for them separately.

BILLY BOB: I mentally figured them in!

BOBBY RAY: No, you didn't. They were drop shipped.

BILLY BOB (*looks at him slightly annoyed*): Good grief. We should have saved some of that padding for your cell.

BOBBY RAY (*innocently*): What do you mean?

BILLY BOB (*still looking at him*): I have a lunatic on my hands!

BOBBY RAY: Well, be careful. Ya got to pull him off your hand slowly or burn him off with a match. If they leave their little teeth in, ya can get infected and that's where ya get that lime disease, ya know. Yup, I had me a tick once right . . . (*starts to gesture to his behind*) well, never mind where, but I got me some burn marks from the match. (*Pauses while* BILLY BOB *continues to stare at him.*) What? Why ya looking at me like that? You still wondering where all the people are?

BILLY BOB (*sarcastically*): No, I'm wondering where you are.

BOBBY RAY: Well, then it's time to get your glasses checked 'cause I'm right here. What'd ya think I was, a figment of your imagination? (*Starts looking at ceiling quizzically*)

BILLY BOB (*sarcastically*): No, but that don't stop me from wishing.

BOBBY RAY (*still looking at ceiling, then realizing*): I got it!

BILLY BOB: Got what?

BOBBY RAY: Why we ain't got no people here! The church! It ain't even finished!

BILLY BOB: What? What do you mean it's not finished?

BOBBY RAY (*standing up to point at the back of congregation*): Look up there! We forgot to complete the second floor so they ain't got no place to sit. (*Laughs*) Well, don't that beat all. Now how'd we go and forget about that?

BILLY BOB (*standing to approach slowly*): Bobby Ray, that there is a balcony, it ain't supposed to be a full floor.

BOBBY RAY (*looking hard*): A balcony? (*Beat, shrugs*) Seems like a waste of space to me. It's sort of like having an elevator that don't go all the way to the top, don't ya think?

BILLY BOB (*sarcastically while looking at him*): You would know.

BOBBY RAY: How'd I know? I ain't got no elevator. (*Pause and sits down*) So do you think they're ever gonna come?

BILLY BOB: The people for our church? I can't rightfully say.

BOBBY RAY: It ain't nothing like Kevin Costner said, is it?

BILLY BOB (*confused*): Kev? What? What's Kevin Costner got to do with anything?

BOBBY RAY: In that movie "Field of Dreams." He said, "If you build it they will come."

BILLY BOB: So?

BOBBY RAY: So we built the church, why didn't the people come like in that movie?

BILLY BOB (*sitting down*): 'Cuz that movie was about baseball. Everyone comes for baseball. Baseball's fun.

BOBBY RAY: Oh, I get it. So people who ain't never been to church before don't know that church is just as fun as baseball, so they don't show up 'cause they ain't never been to church to find out it's fun. (*Beat*) I guess that means we did it backwards.

BILLY BOB: Did what backwards?

BOBBY RAY: We built the church like we was playing baseball in the picture show.

BILLY BOB: What on earth are you talking about?

BOBBY RAY: What you said, church ain't like baseball. It's not "If you build it they will come." It's "If they come, they will build it." We built the church backwards.

BILLY BOB (*thinks for a moment and then slowly realizes*): Ya know, this is the first time that backward thinking of yours might be making sense. Are you saying that with the church we went and got everything and expected the people to come and get it, when really we should have gone and got the people so they could get it themselves?

BOBBY RAY: Yep. (*Beat*) I think that's what I'm saying. (*Beat*) Get what themselves?

BILLY BOB: The Lord! They've got to get Jesus and if they ain't gonna come to church to get Jesus first, then maybe we ought to get Jesus to them to get them to come here and get more!

BOBBY RAY: Oh, yeah!

BOTH: We've got it!

BILLY BOB (*raising hand for a high five*): Slap me!

(BOBBY RAY *raises his hand and hesitates but gently slaps him across the face anyway.*)

BILLY BOB: Ow! Not my face! Slap my hand!

BOBBY RAY: Oh. Sorry.

(BILLY BOB *still has his one hand raised but* BOBBY RAY *grabs* BILLY BOB'S *other hand and slaps it across the back gently with his own hand as if* BOBBY RAY *had been naughty.*)

BILLY BOB: Bobby Ray! (*Stares at* BOBBY RAY *who acts like he knows he did something wrong but he doesn't know what.*) Oh, never mind. (*Drops his hand*) The point is we finally get it.

BOBBY RAY (*nodding in agreement*): Yeah. Getting it's good.

BILLY BOB: Now let's you and me go talk to some folks outside the church so they can get it too. (*Standing up*) You ready?

BOBBY RAY (*standing*): Yup.

BILLY BOB: Good! (*Starts to exit*) Then let's be getting!

(*Exit*)

Rain Men

An "It Just Makes Sense" Sketch

Running Time: 4 minutes

Theme: False boasting

Scripture Reference: "Like clouds and wind without rain is a man who boasts of his gifts falsely." Proverbs 25:14

Cast:
> PA WIMBERLEY—Older gent, loves his wife, isn't afraid to defend himself
> MA WIMBERLEY—Granny type, sweet natured but has a temper if she needs it
> JAKE JACOBS—TV weatherman and neighbor of Ma and Pa
> NARRATOR

Setting: Ma and Pa's back porch. There are two rocking chairs siting side by side. A small toy shotgun is preset on the floor with an afghan to cover it.

Props:
> 2 rocking chairs
> Knitting yarn
> Toy shotgun

Costumes: Pa has overalls and a straw hat on. Ma wears a granny dress. Jake is costumed in a rain coat and rain hat.

(MA and PA enter. MA is carrying her knitting. They both take their seats in the rocking chairs.)

PA: That was a mighty good dinner, Ma.

MA: Thank you, Pa.

PA: Tasted just as good as it did last night when we ate it with our neighbor.

MA: Yes, it did.

PA: Except tonight I liked the company better.

MA: Oh Pa, you say the sweetest things.

JAKE *(offstage)*: Walter Wimberley!

PA: What's that?

JAKE *(offstage)*: Wimberley!

MA: Sounds like someone's at the front door.

PA: Do you wanna get it, Ma?

MA: OK. *(Stands up and takes a few steps and then hollers extremely loud)* We're out back! *(Walks back to her chair and sits down)*

PA: Thanks, Ma.

MA: You're welcome, Pa.

JAKE *(enters)*: Wimberley!

MA: Well, if it isn't our neighbor Jake.

PA: We ain't seen you since last night's supper.

JAKE: That's exactly what I'm here to talk about.

PA: Ya come back for leftovers, huh?

JAKE: No!

MA: Whatcha wearing the rain suit for?

JAKE: That's exactly what I'm here to talk about!

MA: Is it new?

JAKE: No!

PA: Looks nice 'cept it ain't rained all day.

JAKE: That's exactly what I'm here to talk about!

MA: That's the third time he's said that, Pa.

PA: I don't think he knows exactly what he wants to talk about, Ma.

JAKE: Yes, I do! I'm here to talk about the weather.

MA: Well, that's not very original is it, Pa?

PA: He's a TV weatherman, Ma. Sometimes folks get so wrapped up in their work they cain't talk about nuttin' else.

JAKE: Last night, when I was over here for dinner, did you or did you not brag on and on about how your bad right knee can predict the weather?

PA: Well, Jake, I was more stating facts than I was bragging, if you ask me.

MA: No, he's right, Pa. It did sort of sound like bragging.

JAKE: The point is that I believed you! That's exactly why I went on the news this morning wearing this ridiculous get-up and predicting a forecast for the clouds, wind, and rain you said we were going to have.

PA: Ma, didn't we have us some clouds and wind today?

MA: Yes, Pa, we surely did.

JAKE: But we didn't have rain!

PA: So? Two out of three ain't bad.

JAKE: It is if you're in a drought and you get paid to accurately predict the weather! Every farmer in the area must have called the station just to yell at the top of his lungs at me for getting his hopes up.

MA: Good heavens, that must have been rough.

JAKE: Ma'am, you don't know the half of it. My boss is furious with me *(pointing at* PA*)* and it's all his fault!

PA *(angry)*: I don't see what you're hollering and blaming me for! Seems like you should be used to having your boss mad at you. Your satellite pictures only get the weather right half the time anyway!

JAKE: What?

PA: You heard me!

MA: Now, now. I think you both need to settle down.

JAKE: Are you saying my weather predicting ability isn't accurate?

PA: That depends. Are you saying that my weather predicting ability isn't accurate?

MA: OK, you two need to stop it.

JAKE: That's what I'm saying!

PA: Then that's what I'm saying too!

MA: That's enough, boys.

JAKE: Oh yeah?

PA: Yeah!

JAKE: Yeah?

PA: Yeah!

MA *(grabbing toy gun off floor next to her rocking chair, stands up and yells)*: I said stop it! I've done had enough out of both of you! Neither one of you has a right for boasting about predicting rain. The only person who can accurately predict stormy weather around here is me.

PA: What in tarnation are you talking about, Ma?

MA: I got me a gift with my weather stick here *(raises toy gun and points it at them)* and it tells me that if ya both don't stop ruining my night with your arguing, purty soon it's gonna be raining bullets.

JAKE *(pauses and asks* PA*)*: Is she serious?

PA: 'Fraid so. I seen her riled up like this once before, boy, and it wasn't pretty.

JAKE: Really?

PA: How do you think I got my bad knee?

(All actors freeze as NARRATOR *quickly enters, stopping in front of them and facing audience. He has his Bible open.)*

NARRATOR: Proverbs 25:14 says, "Like clouds and wind without rain is a man who boasts of his gifts falsely." *(Slams Bible shut)*

MA: The Bible . . .

PA/JAKE *(in unison)*: it just makes sense. *(All exit quickly.)*

The Weekend of Our Discontent

Running Time: 5 minutes

Theme: The importance of reading the Bible, encouraging each other

Scripture References: "All scripture is inspired by God and profitable for teaching, for reproof, for correction, for training in righteousness; so that the man of God may be adequate, equipped for every good work." 2 Timothy 3:16-17
"Iron sharpens iron, so one man sharpens another." Proverbs 27:17

Cast:
   CHAD
   CHRIS

Setting: Living room

Props:
   Bowl or small bag of pretzels
   2 chairs
   Shoes
   Jacket

Costumes: Contemporary clothing

(CHAD *and* CHRIS *enter room together.* CHAD *doesn't have his shoes on.*)

CHAD: Hey, it's good to see you, man!

CHRIS: It's good to see you too!

CHAD: Come on in and grab a seat.

CHRIS (*heads towards chair*): So both of our wives are away at the women's retreat, huh?

CHAD: Yep. We've got the whole weekend to hang out together.

CHRIS (*sits down*): Sweet.

CHAD (*sits down*): Yeah, nice.

CHRIS (*beat, less enthusiastically*): Sweet.

CHAD (*dragging word out*): Nii-ii-iice. (*Pause*) You don't really want to be here, do you?

CHRIS: No, Cindy made me come. She said Stacey was afraid you'd be lonely with her gone.

CHAD: That's funny. Stacey told me that Cindy wanted you to come over for the same reason.

CHRIS: Women.

CHAD: Even when they're gone they can't leave us alone.

CHRIS: What do they expect us to do together?

CHAD: I don't know. What do women do when they hang out?

CHRIS: Let's see. They go shopping together.

CHAD: Pass.

CHRIS: Work on quilts together.

CHAD: Pass.

CHRIS: Have tea parties together.

CHAD: Pass.

CHRIS: Sometimes they just go to the bathroom together.

CHAD *(looking at him, pauses)*: Definitely pass.

CHRIS: No! I wasn't saying! I was just, you know . . . listing. Making a list. Gimme a break.

CHAD: OK, I've got an idea. Maybe we should just . . . *(struggles to say the next word as though it's not even in his vocabulary)* talk?

CHRIS: Talk, huh?

CHAD: Yeah, talk. Women do that. A lot.

CHRIS: OK.

CHAD: You first.

CHRIS: Nuh-uh. Your idea.

CHAD: Fine. I'll go first then. *(Beat)* So, how's things?

CHRIS: Fine, how's things with you?

CHAD: Good.

CHRIS *(long pause)*: Now what?

CHAD *(shrugs)*: I'm not sure. We just keep talking, I guess.

CHRIS: 'Bout what?

CHAD: I don't know. Things. We talk about things.

CHRIS: But we both just said things were fine.

CHAD: Oh yeah. Things are fine. *(Shrugs)* OK then, we'll talk about stuff.

CHRIS: Stuff?

CHAD: Yeah, stuff. I went first last time. Your turn.

CHRIS: OK. *(Beat)* So . . . do you like stuff?

CHAD: Yeah.

CHRIS: Me too.

CHRIS *(pause)*: So, how much more of this talking stuff do we have to do?

CHAD: I think we're done.

CHRIS: Yep. I'm stuffed. *(Stands up)*

CHAD: You leaving?

CHRIS: Yeah. You know, I can't figure out why those women retreats last an entire weekend.

CHAD *(standing up)*: I know. They'd sure go a lot faster if they'd let men plan it for them.

CHRIS *(notices bowl of pretzels on the table)*: Are those pretzels?

CHAD *(looks at CHRIS, to bowl, back to CHRIS)*: Help yourself.

CHRIS: Nice. Don't mind if I do. *(Grabs some pretzels and sits back down. He stares at the first pretzel before eating it while lost in thought.)* What do you think they're like anyway?

CHAD *(sitting down)*: Pretzels? They're salty. You've never had a pretzel before?

CHRIS: No, not pretzels. A women's retreat. What do you think they're like. *(Eats pretzel)*

CHAD: I don't know. Maybe they just go somewhere and congregate in a really big women's bathroom that seats five hundred people.

CHRIS: Sort of like a stadium that flushes?

CHAD: Exactly. Maybe they rebuilt the Kingdome and called it the Kingthrone.

CHRIS *(thinks about it for a beat while chewing pretzel)*: It's possible I suppose, but doesn't it seem like there'd be more to it than that?

CHAD: Like what?

CHRIS: Well, it's a Christian women's retreat so you'd think that it'd have something to do with being spiritual.

CHAD: Maybe they baptize each other in the sinks.

CHRIS (shrugs): I'll have to ask Cindy when she gets home.

CHAD: Let me know what you find out.

CHRIS: OK. You know, I do kinda miss her.

CHAD: Yeah, I kinda miss my wife too.

(CHRIS and CHAD both continue to eat pretzels throughout the rest of the conversation.)

CHRIS (long pause): Kinda a lot.

CHAD: Ditto. It's sort of cool though when she gets back from one of these retreats, you know?

CHRIS: What do you mean?

CHAD: Well, it helps our marriage when she goes to these things.

CHRIS: Yeah, it helps our marriage when Cindy's gone too. (Beat) I'm kidding.

CHAD (laughs): Good one.

CHRIS: Actually, I'm planning a surprise for her when she gets back.

CHAD: Oh yeah?

CHRIS: Yeah, I'm not gonna be there. (Beat while CHAD looks shocked) I'm kidding again.

CHAD (laughs): Oh.

CHRIS: The truth is that I'm planning to go to the Christian bookstore to get a new couples' devotional or a Bible study for us to do together.

CHAD: You are, huh?

CHRIS: Yep. Then I'm gonna set it on the table with a dozen roses.

CHAD: She'll probably like that.

CHRIS: I'm sure she will. We haven't been as close . . . like . . . spiritually . . . lately, you know? We're both sort of incontinent over it.

CHAD: Incontinent?

CHRIS: Yeah, you know, where you aren't satisfied with how things are in your spiritual life thingy.

CHAD: I think you mean discontent.

CHRIS: Same thing.

CHAD: Not really.

CHRIS: Anyway, I think that's why she was so excited about the retreat.

CHAD: Oh.

CHRIS: How about you and Stacey?

CHAD: How about me and Stacey, what?

CHRIS: You know, are you guys close?

CHAD: To God? Oh yeah. We're close. We're content. We're rock solid. We're great. We're doing . . . about the same as you.

CHRIS: That bad, eh?

CHAD: Could be better.

CHRIS: You should do a Bible study together.

CHAD: Yeah?

CHRIS: It makes a difference. I mean it shows up in both Cindy and I when we're not reading the Bible. You know what I mean?

CHAD: Sort of. You guys do a Bible study together all the time or something?

CHRIS: That or a devotional. We finished the last one a couple months ago but we've both been so busy we haven't gotten a new one since. I'm planning to fix that before she gets home. Gotta get back on track.

CHAD: It helps that much, huh?

CHRIS: It keeps us both on the same page spiritually, so to speak.

Chad: Maybe I ought to go with you and get one for Stacey and me.

CHRIS: Sounds good. You wanna go with me to get one now?

CHAD: Sure, I could use getting out of the house. *(Gets up to get his shoes)* Let me get my shoes and jacket.

CHRIS: OK. We should stop at the grocery store on the way back also.

CHAD: For what?

CHRIS *(holds up bowl)*: You're out of pretzels. *(Laughs)* Sorry.

CHAD *(sits back down to put shoes on)*: You mind if I steal your idea and get her a dozen roses while we're at the store too?

CHRIS: Help yourself.

CHAD: Nice.

CHRIS: So, what are you gonna do the rest of the weekend with Stacey gone?

CHAD *(putting shoes on)*: I don't know. Run through the house with scissors. Eat with my mouth open. Talk with it full. Maybe I'll just take all my underwear and socks out of the dresser and leave them on the bedroom floor for the weekend. You know . . . stuff.

CHRIS: Sounds like fun, but you'd better pick the clothes back up before she returns.

CHAD: Naw, I'll leave them there so she feels wanted when she gets home. *(Stands up, grabbing jacket)*

CHRIS *(standing up, laughing)*: You're kidding.

CHAD *(beat, seriously)*: No.

CHRIS *(pauses, looking at CHAD)*: You'd better get two dozen roses. *(Beat)* Come on.

(They exit.)

Addicted, to You

An "It Just Makes Sense" Sketch

Running Time: 4 minutes

Theme: Judging others

Scripture Reference: "Why do you look at the speck that is in your brother's eye, but do not notice the log that is in your own eye?" Matthew 7:3

Cast:
> FRANK—Big brother, easy going, sensible, patient to a point
> SARAH—Little sister, concerned, emotional, dramatic
> NARRATOR

Setting: City park

Props:
> Park bench

Costumes: Contemporary clothing

(FRANK *is seated on the bench and looks at his watch while waiting for* SARAH. *She enters.*)

SARAH: Hi, how's my favorite brother doing?

FRANK: Great, thanks. And you?

SARAH (*sitting on bench*): I'm great too.

FRANK: Whew, that's a relief. I was worried.

SARAH: Worried?

FRANK: Yeah. Your message said you wanted to meet in the park today to discuss something important.

SARAH: Oh that. Well, you can stop worrying. I'm fine. In fact, it's not even me that I wanted to discuss. It's you.

FRANK (*innocently*): Oh? What is it?

SARAH: Well, there's no nice way to say this so I'll just say it. (*Takes deep breath*) I think you're an addict.

FRANK (*laughs and thinks she's joking*): A what?

SARAH: An addict.

FRANK (*tries to laugh it off*): You're kidding me, right?

SARAH: No.

FRANK (*getting serious but playing along*): I see. And I'm addicted to . . . ?

SARAH: Sports.

FRANK: Sports?

SARAH: Yep. You watch sports all the time and that makes you an addict.

FRANK: Gimme a break. I watch what, maybe one game a week?

SARAH: Oh come on, Frank. You watch a lot more than that. Every time I come over to visit you and Margaret you're always glued to your television set watching a game.

FRANK: That's because you only come over to visit on Saturdays and that's usually the day that my game is on.

SARAH: Clearly you're in denial. That's OK. In fact it's typical. Heather had to work through denial too before she finally got help with her addiction.

FRANK: Heather, who?

SARAH: Rossmore. She had an addiction to gambling.

FRANK: Heather Rossmore?

SARAH: Yes, she's a friend of mine. Or at least she was until she died. (*Tearing up*) I'm sorry, but I get emotional whenever I think about it.

FRANK: Wow. I feel like a bad brother. I didn't even know you had a friend named Heather.

SARAH: Well, maybe if you weren't so wrapped up in your sports you would.

FRANK: I'm not wrapped up in . . . (*realizing she is emotional, lets her comment slide*) Never mind. (*Pause*) So how'd she die?

SARAH (*sniffling*): Eye infection.

FRANK: She died from an eye infection?

SARAH: No, she drove off a cliff but she was on her way to get her eye infection looked at when it happened. Listen, I can't to talk about it right now. It's still too fresh. It just happened yesterday. (*Becoming more tearful*)

FRANK: Yesterday? (*Puts his arm around her to comfort her*) Man, I'm sorry, sis. I didn't know.

SARAH (*crying*): She didn't even get to meet the son she never knew she had.

FRANK: She didn't know she had a son?

SARAH (*wiping her eyes and regaining control*): A bear ate her first husband when

Heather was pregnant, but then aliens abducted the baby after Heather gave birth.

FRANK *(pulls away to look at her)*: What?

SARAH: I know, it's awful! And then the aliens brainwashed Heather so she'd forget and now . . . *(wailing)* she's deeeeeaaaaad!

FRANK *(concerned she is going crazy)*: Sarah . . . umm . . . are you all right?

SARAH *(sniffles)*: Not really, but I'm sure I'll get over it with time.

FRANK *(truly concerned)*: No, I mean are you all right in your mind? Are you sure about all of this?

SARAH: Of course I'm sure. *(Beat)* Or at least I think I am. Although they never actually showed Heather's body so I suppose she could be alive. *(Pause)* Oh my word. I'll bet that's it! She really is alive! Colonel Mordell probably pushed the car off the cliff and faked her death! Then he kidnapped her so he could hold Heather captive on his island until she returns his unrequited love.

FRANK: What on earth are you talking about?

SARAH: Heather Rossmore on *As the World Burns*! It's my favorite soap opera. It's on right after *All My Sins*, *The Blinding Light* and the *Stupid and the Shameful*. I watch them every day.

FRANK: You watch four hours of soap opera's every single day?

SARAH: Well, not *every* day. They don't air on weekends.

FRANK *(getting angry)*: And you call me an addict?

SARAH: Is there a problem?

FRANK *(angry)*: The problem is that I'm not an addict! I gave up watching a game today just to meet you!

SARAH: You did?

FRANK: Yes!

SARAH *(shrugs indifferently)*: Oh. Well, then maybe you aren't an addict.

FRANK: That's what I'm saying! I'm not an addict, you are!

SARAH: Oh please, spare me the melodrama. I'm not an addict. I just like my shows. You're completely overreacting.

FRANK *(fed up and angry)*: You stage this little intervention in the park and call me a sports addict just because I watch one game on Saturdays and I'm the one who's overreacting? Me? I'm the overreactor? Is that what I'm doing? I'm overreacting?

SARAH *(passing judgment)*: That's right, and if you ask me, someone's been watching too many soap operas.

(Actors freeze as NARRATOR quickly enters, stopping in front of them, facing audience. He has his Bible open.)

NARRATOR: When it comes to passing judgment on others, Matthew 7:3 says, "Why do you look at the speck that is in your brother's eye, but do not notice the log that is in your own eye?" *(Slams Bible shut)* The Bible . . .

FRANK/NARRATOR: It just makes sense.

(Actors exit quickly.)

Knowing You

Running Time: 4 minutes

Theme: God knows us

Scripture Reference: "O Lord, you have searched me and known me. You know when I sit down and when I rise up; You understand my thoughts from afar. You scrutinize my path and my lying down, and are intimately acquainted with all my ways. Even before there is a word on my tongue, behold, O Lord, You know it all." Psalm 139:1-6

Cast:
JOHN—Loving husband, nice guy, sense of humor, quiet at times
WENDY—Loving wife, sense of humor and somewhat of a talker

Setting: Back porch

Props:
Bench

Costumes: Contemporary wear

(JOHN *is seated on the bench and is deep in thought.* WENDY *enters.*)

WENDY: OK, everyone is gone and I'm done cleaning up.

JOHN: Good. Want to take a break and sit out here with me?

WENDY: Don't mind if I do. *(Sitting down)* Hey, next time I want to throw a dinner party, do me a favor and remind me how exhausting it is.

JOHN: Done deal. *(Pause as* JOHN *stares at the sky)*

WENDY *(looks at* JOHN *and realizes he is lost in thought)*: So what's on your mind?

JOHN: What do you mean?

WENDY: Come on, I know that look.

JOHN: Naw. It's nothing really.

WENDY: John?

JOHN *(laughs)*: OK, I give up. I'm just thinking about something that happened at the party.

WENDY: What?

JOHN: Well, it's kind of funny actually, but it felt like every time I tried to talk you'd jump in and . . .

WENDY: Finish your sentences?

JOHN: That's it exactly. I'm not really bothered by it though. I was just . . .

WENDY: Thinking about it.

JOHN *(looks at her scoldingly)*: Right.

WENDY *(laughs)*: I'm sorry! *(Becoming serious)* Believe it or not, I'm actually aware that I do that to you. I even try to control it but it's just that . . .

JOHN: You know me so well . . .

WENDY: And I get excited about telling a story so I want to . . .

JOHN: Finish it for me.

WENDY *(beat)*: You do it too, you know.

JOHN: What?

WENDY: Finish my sentences. You just did it twice.

JOHN *(laughs)*: I know. It's just that I'm more aware of it . . .

WENDY: When I finish yours.

JOHN: Anyway, that's what I was thinking about. I told you it wasn't anything major. It's just that it's a little . . .

WENDY: Annoying when somebody finishes your sentences?

JOHN: Yes.

JOHN/WENDY *(in unison)*: You've/I've got to try to learn to control that.

JOHN *(laughs)*: Good luck.

WENDY *(laughs)*: Right back at ya. *(Beat)* You know, when you think about it though, it kind of works to our benefit.

JOHN: Knowing each other so well?

WENDY: Yeah. We know when one of us is in a bad mood . . .

JOHN: Or thinking . . .

WENDY: Or hungry . . .

JOHN: Or sad . . .

WENDY: Or tired . . .

JOHN: So we always know how to take care of each other.

WENDY: Yep, we even know when one of us wants to be left alone.

JOHN *(beat)*: No. You don't know that one.

WENDY (*laughs*): Trust me. I know it. I just choose to ignore it. (*Beat*) Kind of like God.

JOHN: Huh? Oh, I get it. Yeah, you're right. He doesn't ignore us when we want to be left alone either.

WENDY: There's no escaping Him. But then again, who'd want to? I actually take comfort knowing He knows me. (*Laughing suddenly*) I just thought of something.

JOHN: What?

WENDY: Well, can you imagine if God was at a dinner party? He knows everything so He'd be finishing everyone's sentences!

JOHN (*laughs*): Or if you were trying to tell Him a story about your past? You'd be like, "So God, did I ever tell you about the time that . . . oh yeah . . . You were there." (*Both laugh*)

WENDY (*pause*): Seriously though, I think God is the only person who knows either of us better than we know each other.

JOHN: He probably knew we were going to have this conversation before we even had it.

JOHN/WENDY (*both pause, look upward to heaven and then turn to each other and say in unison*): Now that's annoying! (*Both look upward toward heaven again to apologize to God.*) Sorry.

WENDY: There are certain benefits to God knowing us so well.

JOHN: Yeah, it's nice to have someone who knows what I'm talking about when I'm complaining about you.

WENDY: John!

JOHN: Gotcha!

WENDY: That's OK, God and I share some really good inside jokes about you so we're even.

JOHN: What?

WENDY: Gotcha!

JOHN (*laughs while standing up*): Good one. (*Beat*) You ready to . . . (*offers her his hand*)

WENDY (*accepts his hand and gets up*): Go in? Yeah. I'm feeling . . .

JOHN: Tired. Me too.

WENDY (*holding JOHN's hand she looks upward to say good night to God*): Good night, God. Thanks for giving us such a great evening.

JOHN (*looking upward too*): Yeah. Thanks, God. It's nice knowing Ya.

WENDY (*pointing to sky*): Honey, look!

JOHN: A shooting star.

WENDY (*quietly in awe*): Wow. It's beautiful.

JOHN (*to WENDY*): You know what I think?

WENDY (*looks at JOHN*): What?

JOHN: I think that was God's way of saying it's nice knowing us too.

(*They both start to exit while holding hands. WENDY is still looking upward.*)

WENDY (*looking upward*): Nice.

(*Exit*)